Classifications of political ideas

Q1 Distinguish between 'left-wing' and 'right-wing' political ideas.

Q2 Why do some contemporary political commentators — and politicians — argue that the 'left/right' model of political ideas is outdated?

Q3 Distinguish between the 'organic' and the 'mechanistic' models of society.

ANSWERS

A1 Very basically, 'right-wing' attitudes support and defend the existing system, while 'left-wing' thinkers seek progressive changes. Right-wing philosophies usually favour private economic ownership and social hierarchy, while left-wing theories favour varying degrees of common economic ownership and social equality (see also Number 2).

A2 The current decade has witnessed a sustained period of consensus politics with the main parties pursuing various blends of political centrism, e.g. a 'third way' or 'compassionate conservatism'.

A3 The 'organic' model of society perceives the state to be more important than the individual. The 'mechanistic' model asserts the primacy of the individual.

***examiner's* note** None of the forms of classification, alone, is adequate to locate and understand every political ideology.

ANSWERS

Left and right wing

Q1 How do 'left' and 'right' schools of political thought view human nature?

Q2 What is meant by 'reactionary' political views?

Q3 How do 'left' and 'right' political theories view the state?

ANSWERS

A1 Left-wingers are optimists about human nature, viewing it as social and altruistic. Right-wingers are pessimists, viewing human nature as irrational and selfish.

A2 A desire to return to a previous situation, or to go back in time, is called 'reactionary'.

A3 Left-wing systems vary from the strong and oppressive Stalinist model to the small, stateless, self-governing and egalitarian economic collectives envisaged by Marx and by left-wing anarchist theories. Similarly, right-wing private ownership may take the form of extreme *laissez faire* and limited government, or of totalitarian fascism with an all-powerful state.

***examiner's* note** Many political doctrines, such as nationalism and feminism, attach themselves to various wider political ideologies and, in so doing, adopt different 'left' or 'right' perspectives in the process.

 ANSWERS

Human nature

Q1 What is the left-wing view of human nature?

Q2 What is the right-wing, organic view of human nature?

Q3 What is the individualist view of human nature?

ANSWERS ▶▶

A1 Left-wing, collectivist theories, such as socialism, generally believe that humans have a social and altruistic core and that they work better as cooperative groups than as selfish individuals — but that human nature is strongly influenced by its environment, i.e. is 'plastic'. Philosophically, they usually favour limited or no state and government.

A2 Right-wing, organic theories, such as conservatism and fascism, have profound doubts about both human rationality and human goodness. Therefore they usually favour a strong state.

A3 Individualist philosophies, such as liberalism, generally believe that humans are rational, but in a selfish way.

***examiner's* note** A political ideology's view of human nature is often central to an explanation of its wider views about state and society.

 3 ANSWERS

Origins and role of the state

Q1 Define the 'state'.

Q2 Outline the organic theory of the state.

Q3 Outline the mechanistic theory of the state.

ANSWERS

A1 The 'state' is the abstract, permanent, sovereign political power over a given territory, embracing legislative, executive and judicial functions.

A2 The organic theory likens the state to a living organism with its parts unequal and interdependent. The state is more important than any individual within it. There is a natural, harmonious hierarchy within the state. Traditional conservatism and fascism are organic theories.

A3 The mechanistic theory holds that the state is like an artificial machine, created by man to serve man, and therefore the individual is the unit of primary importance. Liberalism and New Right economic conservatism (*laissez faire*) are mechanistic theories.

***examiner's* note** Some ideologies — notably left-wing, anti-statist theories such as communism and left-wing anarchism — cannot be categorised on the organic/mechanistic model at all.

Power

Q1 Why do some political philosophies reject democracy?

Q2 What is meant by 'oligarchy'?

Q3 List three forms of oligarchy.

ANSWERS

A1 Philosophies with a pessimistic view of human goodness or rationality reject the view that the mass of humans can be trusted with decision-making power.

A2 'Oligarchy' means rule by the few, or elitism. Direct democracy is rule by the many in its purest form, whereas representative democracy is a form of oligarchy.

A3 • Aristocracy: rule by the 'best', whether the most able, noble or wealthy etc.
• Meritocracy: rule by the most skilled, trained and able
• Technocracy: rule by technical experts, scientists and engineers

***examiner's* note** Organic theories, and those with a pessimistic view of human nature, invariably advocate elitist power structures. Egalitarian theories, and those with an optimistic view of human nature, invariably advocate democracy.

 ANSWERS

The 'graph' model

Q1 Describe the 'graph' model of political ideologies.

Q2 Why was the 'graph' model devised?

Q3 Give one example of a right-wing political ideology that advocates a strong state; and one example of a right-wing political ideology that advocates a weak state.

ANSWERS

A1 The 'graph' model charts left-wing versus right-wing political ideologies on the horizontal axis, with those ideologies that advocate a strong state versus those advocating a weak or no state on the central vertical axis.

A2 The 'left/right' classification is essentially an economic one: it separates egalitarians from elitists. Both left-wingers and right-wingers, however, may believe in either a strong, authoritarian state to enforce their policies, or a weak and limited state to enhance citizens' freedom. There is no necessary connection between 'left/right' and a 'strong/weak' state.

A3 Fascism; anarcho-capitalism.

***examiner's* note** The 'graph' model produces a rather more complex, sophisticated and helpful model of political ideas than the somewhat one-dimensional 'left/right' classification.

Strong state

	Left wing		Right wing
	Stalinism	Fascism	
	Marxism	Anarcho-capitalism	

Weak/no state

(6) **ANSWERS**

The concept of 'ideology'

Q1 Who originally devised the concept of 'ideology'?

Q2 Explain the original meaning of the word 'ideology'.

Q3 In what sense is this usage positive?

ANSWERS

A1 The term 'ideology' was originally devised by Antoine Destutt de Tracy (1754–1836), an aristocrat and philosopher of the French Enlightenment (*Éléments d'idéologie*, 1801).

A2 It originally meant the general 'science of ideas'. De Tracy sought to combine psychology and biology in order to analyse the nature of human consciousness.

A3 This was a positive usage of the word 'ideology' in so far as it favoured the belief that human ideas themselves could be studied in an objective and scientific way.

***examiner's* note** 'Ideology' is often cited as the most contested and yet the most frequently utilised concept in politics. This is because the word 'ideology' has been used in many different ways by different political thinkers, for different motives.

 (7) **ANSWERS**

The neutral usage of the concept 'ideology'

Q1 Which writer is mainly associated with the neutral usage of the concept 'ideology'?

Q2 Explain the neutral usage of the concept 'ideology'.

Q3 How is this usage employed in political theory?

ANSWERS

A1 Martin Seliger (*Politics and Ideology*, 1976).

A2 An 'ideology' is a set or system of related ideas, beliefs and values that may be used to understand and interpret events, and to guide and direct actions towards specified aims.

A3 An examination syllabus centring on 'political ideologies' is clearly employing the term 'ideology' in this neutral sense, but will involve analysis of the concept in all of its diverse usages, including the positive and the negative.

***examiner's* note** By this usage any '-ism' — such as communism, fascism, conservatism or anarchism — is an ideology, and no value judgements are being made about whether each is good or bad.

Negative usages
of the concept 'ideology'

Q1 Explain the Marxist usage of 'ideology'.

Q2 Explain the liberal usage of 'ideology'.

Q3 Explain the conservative usage of 'ideology'.

ANSWERS

A1 For Marxism, 'ideology' refers to the set of ideas and values that reflect and protect the interests of an economic ruling class. Since Marxism opposes all class structures, it opposes ideology; and as objective 'scientific socialism', Marxism cannot be ideology by its own definition.

A2 For liberalism, 'ideology' means polarised and extremist ideas of the radical left and radical right. Since liberalism dislikes extremism, it opposes ideology.

A3 For conservatism, 'ideology' means any abstract theory. Since conservatism mistrusts human rationality and humans' capacity to theorise, it opposes ideology.

***examiner's* note** All of these can be argued to be ideological in one or more senses of the word — even if only in the neutral sense employed by Seliger (see Number 8).

9 **ANSWERS**

The 'end of ideology'

Q1 Which writer is associated with the 'end of ideology' thesis?

Q2 What is meant by the 'end of ideology'?

Q3 Explain why the 'end of ideology' thesis has been proven wrong.

ANSWERS

A1 Daniel Bell (*The End of Ideology*, 1960).

A2 In the economic boom after the Second World War some political commentators perceived a growth in 'consensus politics', with the main parties shedding many of their ideological differences, converging towards the centre of the political spectrum and advocating similar policies of Keynesian welfarism.

A3 The 1980s saw economic recession and the polarisation of the main political parties in a new era of 'adversary politics', and the 1990s onwards saw the world torn apart by nationalist and religious conflicts. Radicalism clearly was not dead.

examiner's **note** The last decade witnessed a new, if more right-wing, 'end of ideology' between the two main UK political parties — at least until economic recession.

Classical liberalism

Q1 What is the liberal view of human nature?

Q2 Define 'individualism' and explain its importance within liberal ideology.

Q3 Describe the economic system favoured by classical liberals.

ANSWERS

A1 Liberals view human nature as rational but self-interested — an ambivalent view that helps to explain many other liberal doctrines.

A2 'Individualism' is a belief in the primacy of the human individual over any group, society or state. For liberals, this means giving priority to the rights and interests of the individual; it underpins liberal beliefs in freedom, toleration, foundational and formal equality, limited government and representative democracy.

A3 Classical liberals believed in *laissez-faire* (literally 'leave-alone') economics: free-market, private-enterprise capitalism based on 'negative freedom', i.e. non-interference, especially by the state.

***examiner's* note** Classical liberal ideas have been revived since the 1970s in the form of neo-liberalism, which has been adopted by right-wing conservatives within the New Right.

Modern liberalism

Q1 What is the main difference between classical liberalism and modern liberalism?

Q2 What is meant by 'positive freedom'?

Q3 What are the implications of positive freedom for the role of the state?

ANSWERS

A1 Modern liberalism came to perceive that the classical liberal belief in negative freedom and 'survival of the fittest' in the free market may penalise individuals who, through no fault of their own, lack the health, education or skills to thrive unaided. It therefore redefined 'equal opportunity' and the role of the state in the economy.

A2 'Positive individual freedom' is the actualised freedom to fulfil one's own potential and achieve personal development and self-realisation.

A3 Positive freedom implies, where necessary, a positive and empowering role for the state in a mixed-market economy providing health, welfare and education to help individuals make the most of themselves.

examiner's **note** Modern liberalism is sometimes also known as 'social liberalism' or 'welfare liberalism'.

Negative and positive freedom

Q1 Why did classical liberals favour negative freedom?

Q2 Give one or more quotations in support of this view.

Q3 Why did modern liberals reject *laissez-faire* economics?

ANSWERS ▶▶

A1 Classical liberals favoured freedom from external interference of any sort, especially by government and state, because they believed that rational and self-interested individuals were capable of flourishing best in a free-market economy. Economic inequality should be an incentive to enterprise.

A2 • 'That government is best which governs least' (Thomas Jefferson, 1802)
   • 'Heaven helps those who help themselves' (Samuel Smiles, 1859)
   • 'The drunk in the gutter is just where he ought to be' (William Sumner, 1884)

A3 Modern liberals came to perceive that free-market capitalism sets up barriers to genuine freedom for those who are disadvantaged by poverty, sickness and ignorance.

***examiner's* note** Modern liberals continue to favour negative freedom in the private sphere of home, family and personal morality.

Classical versus modern liberalism

Q1 How do classical and modern liberals differ in their views of individualism?

Q2 How do classical and modern liberals differ in their views of freedom?

Q3 How do classical and modern liberals differ in their views of the state?

ANSWERS

A1 Classical liberals believe in egoistical individualism, implying atomism and self-interest; modern liberals embrace the doctrine of developmental individualism that gives priority to human flourishing and takes account of altruistic (generous) as well as egoistical (selfish) sensibilities.

A2 Classical liberals believe in negative economic freedom, whereas modern liberals believe in positive freedom (see Numbers 11–13).

A3 Classical liberals support a minimal state that provides only security and order, while modern liberals view state intervention more positively, believing that it can enlarge and not merely lessen freedom. Thus, whereas classical liberals endorsed the free market, modern liberals advocate a mixed economy and favour social reform and welfare.

examiner's **note** Modern liberals have redefined freedom and hence the proper role of the state.

 ANSWERS

Modern liberal dilemmas

Q1 Why does the liberal view of human nature pose philosophical dilemmas?

Q2 Why does the liberal view of the state pose philosophical dilemmas?

Q3 Why does the liberal view of freedom pose philosophical dilemmas?

ANSWERS

A1 Liberals view humans as rational and therefore deserving of freedom, but also as selfish and therefore corruptible by power; hence people's freedom to acquire excessive power must be curbed.

A2 Liberals view the state as a necessary evil: necessary to safeguard law, order, security and positive freedom, but evil because it is a sovereign power and therefore inherently oppressive. How far does the proper role of the state extend before it stops enhancing freedom and starts becoming coercive?

A3 One person's freedom is another's constraint; for example, one person's social welfare is another person's taxation.

***examiner's* note** Many examination essay questions centre on these and other tensions within modern liberal theory — for example, liberals' qualified support for equality.

Liberal democracy —
a contradictory concept?

Q1 What is the main contradiction between liberalism and democracy?

Q2 Why might democracy threaten minority rights and interests?

Q3 Summarise the potential contradictions between liberalism and democracy.

ANSWERS

A1 Liberalism is individualist, whereas democracy is a collectivist concept.

A2 Democracy implies 'tyranny of the majority'.

A3

Liberalism		Democracy
Individualist		Collectivist
Supports minority rights		Majoritarian
In favour of property rights		Threatens property rights
Favours freedom		Favours equality
Wary of state	versus	Leans to statism
Supports economic freedom and growth		Supports economic stability and welfarism
Rationalist		Demagogic
Believes power corrupts		Believes in 'people power'

examiner's note All liberals are inherently wary of 'people power'.

Liberal democracy — compatibilities

Q1 Why did liberals come to accept democracy?

Q2 How may democracy safeguard freedom?

Q3 What is meant by 'liberal democracy'?

ANSWERS

A1 Democracy seeks to ensure that government rests on the consent of the people and therefore possesses legitimate authority. It also helps to keep government responsive to public opinion and ultimately holds it to account for its actions. A liberal democratic system therefore helps to ensure both representative and responsible government.

A2 Democracy also serves as a means of defending the individual from over-powerful government, by providing checks and constraints against the government.

A3 'Liberal democracy' is a system of individual representation and protection of individual rights based on free, regular and competitive elections, constitutionalism and the rule of law.

***examiner's* note** Modern liberals have come to embrace democracy, but only in its specifically liberal form.

Liberal democracy in the UK

Q1 What 'liberal' features should the UK political system exhibit?

Q2 What factors limit the liberal features of the UK political system?

Q3 What 'democratic' features should the UK political system exhibit?

Q4 What factors limit the democratic features of the UK political system?

ANSWERS

A1 The UK political system should embody constitutionalism, the rule of law, separation of powers, civil liberties and tolerance.

A2 The UK does not have a codified constitution. Parliament and government are fused rather than separate. Critics argue that the UK is becoming a 'surveillance society'.

A3 The UK political system should embody pluralism, consent, political equality, representation of individual voters and accountability of government.

A4 The Westminster Parliament is — at best — a two-party system. 'One person, one vote, one *value*' is negated by wasted votes in the first-past-the-post electoral system. 'Elective dictatorship' — the power of a majority government in Parliament — often limits the accountability of government.

***examiner's* note** The UK is a defective liberal democracy.

The UK Liberal Democrat Party

Q1 When was the Liberal Party formed?

Q2 When and why did the Liberal Democrat Party form?

Q3 What are the main values and principles of the Liberal Democrat Party today?

ANSWERS

A1 The original Liberal Party was formed in the mid-nineteenth century.

A2 The Liberal Democrat Party emerged out of the break-up of the SDP/Liberal Alliance after the 1987 election and the merger of most of its members under the leadership of Paddy Ashdown.

A3 The Liberal Democrats favour a largely private enterprise economy but with positive state intervention to promote positive individual freedom through the provision of qualified welfare. They strongly support civil liberties and issues of constitutional reform — notably a written constitution and Bill of Rights, proportional representation, devolution or federalism, a democratic second chamber and a federal Europe.

examiner's **note** The Liberal Democrats are disadvantaged by the first-past-the-post electoral system at Westminster, which generates a two-party system.

 19 **ANSWERS**

Liberal influences on the other major UK ideologies and parties

Q1 Which doctrines has the Conservative Party adopted from liberal philosophy?

Q2 Which doctrines has the Labour Party adopted from liberal philosophy?

Q3 What are the exceptions to this liberal influence upon UK politics?

ANSWERS

A1 The Conservative Party, through Thatcherism, has adopted the free-market economics and atomistic individualism of classical liberalism — i.e. neo-liberalism.

A2 'New' Labour has adopted a liberal form of communitarianism, where emphasis on widening individual rights and entitlements is balanced against the importance of social duty and moral responsibility. Its welfare reform policies have been influenced by this rights and responsibilities agenda. New Labour's constitutional reforms are — in diluted form — derived largely from constitutional liberalism with its belief in decentralising and fragmenting power.

A3 New Labour (as well as the Conservative Party) has pursued an illiberal programme of authoritarian policies on law and order and anti-terrorism.

***examiner's* note** The liberal influence upon UK politics and parties has been partial and paradoxical.

Traditional conservatism

Q1 Who is widely seen as the founding father of traditional conservatism?

Q2 What are the two main doctrines of traditional conservatism?

Q3 Why do traditional conservatives value tradition?

ANSWERS

A1 Edmund Burke (1729–97).

A2 The two main doctrines of traditional conservatism are the organic view of state and society (see Number 4); and a pessimistic view of human nature as psychologically, intellectually and morally imperfect.

A3 Traditional customs are part of the natural organic order, and can even be regarded as 'God-given'. They have been tested by time and reflect the accumulated wisdom of the past — the 'democracy of the dead' (G. K. Chesterton); and they give psychologically imperfect humans a sense of rootedness and identity. 'That which has stood the test of time is good and should not be lightly cast aside' (Burke).

examiner's **note** Organicism and a belief in human imperfection explain all other conservative doctrines.

Tory paternalism

Q1 What is meant by 'paternalism', and with which Conservative leader is it associated?

Q2 Why is it also often called 'one-nation' conservatism?

Q3 What are the policy implications of paternalism?

ANSWERS

A1 Traditional conservative 'paternalism' means benign authority exercised by the 'natural governors' to guide, aid and support those below. It was first adopted by Benjamin Disraeli (1804–81).

A2 Disraeli feared the destabilising consequences of growing economic inequality and the emergence of 'two nations': the rich and the poor. He foresaw the need to stave off revolution: 'If the cottages are happy, the castle is safe.'

A3 Tory paternalism therefore implies the acceptance of welfarism, whether through church, voluntary organisations or the state.

***examiner's* note** Tory paternalist welfarism is motivated by both principle — social compassion — and pragmatism — a self-interested desire to preserve the status quo, and the dominant position of the 'natural' elite, by damping down social unrest among the lower orders.

Tory pragmatism

Q1 What is meant by 'pragmatism'?

Q2 How does Tory pragmatism relate to the traditional conservative view of human nature?

Q3 How does this stance help to explain the traditional conservative rejection of 'ideology'?

ANSWERS

A1 'Pragmatism' means a practical, flexible and limited response to concrete, changing circumstances, eschewing abstract or rigid theories and doctrines.

A2 Traditional conservatism believes that human beings are intellectually imperfect. The world is too complex for them to explain rationally and understand, and abstract theories and principles are therefore distrusted. Tradition, experience and pragmatism are the surest guides to human action.

A3 Traditional conservatism therefore claims that it is not an 'ideology' in the neutral sense (Seliger) of a comprehensive package of abstract principles and doctrines (see Number 8).

***examiner's* note** Although conservatism is pragmatic, it does have identifiable theoretical doctrines and principles, such as: the organic theory; mistrust of human reason; and pragmatism.

(23) ANSWERS

New Right
neo-liberalism

Q1 Explain briefly the origins of New Right neo-liberalism.

Q2 Outline the main doctrines of neo-liberalism.

Q3 Why does neo-liberalism advocate limited government and state?

ANSWERS ⟩⟩

A1 The origins of neo-liberalism lie in eighteenth-century classical liberalism, but it came to dominate conservative thinking across much of Europe and America in the 1980s.

A2 Neo-liberalism is based upon a belief in human nature as rational and self-seeking, and hence in atomistic individualism and support for a free-market economy.

A3 New-liberalism believes:
- The individual has primacy over the state
- Human nature is rational and deserving of freedom from the state
- The 'invisible hand' of the market generates economic equilibrium
- State taxes, rules and bureaucracy limit personal enterprise and freedom
- High public spending creates inflation
- Excessive state welfare generates a 'dependency culture'

***examiner's* note** New Right neo-liberalism contrasts profoundly with traditional conservatism. This is the theme of many essay questions.

New Right
neo-conservatism

Q1 Explain briefly the origins of New Right neo-conservatism.

Q2 Outline the main doctrines of neo-conservatism.

Q3 What is the main difference between traditional conservatism and neo-conservatism?

ANSWERS

A1 New Right conservatism (or 'Thatcherism' in the UK) has two distinct theoretical strands within it: neo-liberalism (see Number 24) and neo-conservatism. New Right neo-conservatism derives from a highly disciplinarian school of organic conservatism that predates Disraelian paternalism.

A2 Neo-conservatives are authoritarian, disciplinarian and illiberal. Their solution to social unrest is strict and punitive law and order, and a return to traditional values of family, Christian morality and national strength and unity. They dislike immigration, multiculturalism and internationalism. This strand is also strongly Eurosceptic.

A3 Whereas traditional conservatism is benign and paternalist, neo-conservatism is authoritarian and punitive.

examiner's **note** American neo-conservatives are notable for their attachment to Christian fundamentalism, but UK neo-conservatives are less morally doctrinaire.

(25) **ANSWERS**

```
                        Conservatism
            ┌───────────────────┴───────────────────┐
    Traditional                              New Right
    conservatism              ┌──────────────────┴──────────────────┐
                        Neo-liberalism                    Neo-conservatism
```

Organic	Mechanistic	Organic
Mistrusts human nature	Rationalist	Mistrusts human nature
Political/social	Economic	Political/social
Traditional	Radical/reactionary	Reactionary
Natural governors	Meritocratic	Natural governors
Paternalist	*Laissez faire*	Authoritarian
Pragmatic	Principled	Principled

All conservatives believe in private property, hierarchy, law and
order, and traditional family values, although in different ways an
for different reasons.

aminer's note To these contrasting conservative philosophies must be
ed David Cameron's 'modern, compassionate conservatism' in the UK
Number 30).

The New Right 'paradox'

Q1 What is a paradox?

Q2 What is the main contradiction within New Right theory?

Q3 Summarise the main contradictions between New Right
neo-liberalism and neo-conservatism.

A1 A paradox is a contradiction. There are some fundamental contradictions between New Right neo-liberalism and New Right neo-conservatism.

A2 In the economic sphere, New Right neo-liberalism advocates negative freedom from state intervention. In the social, moral and political spheres, however, New Right neo-conservatism is illiberal and favours a strong and controlling state, especially in law and order.

A3 Main contradictions:
- Neo-liberal mechanistic theory versus neo-conservative organic theory
- Rationalism versus mistrust of human nature
- Belief in negative economic freedom versus illiberalism
- Belief in equal opportunity versus anti-egalitarianism
- Belief in limited state versus belief in strong state

examiner's note New Right theory is paradoxical because it combines liberal and conservative philosophies.

Comparisons and contrasts within conservatism

Q1 Summarise the main comparisons and contrasts within conservative philosophy.

Q2 What common beliefs are shared by all conservatives (if in different ways)?

ex
add
(se

ANS\

2

The UK Conservative Party pre-1979

Q1 Outline briefly the origins of the UK Conservative Party.

Q2 When, during the twentieth century, was Disraelian paternalism resurrected?

Q3 When did New Right Thatcherism emerge?

ANSWERS

A1 The origins of the UK Conservative Party lie in the Tory faction of late-seventeenth-century monarchists. In its modern form it dates from 1834, when Robert Peel's Tamworth Manifesto combined a defence of traditional institutions with a programme of moderate reforms.

A2 In the postwar period until the 1970s, the Conservatives pursued Harold Macmillan's 'middle way', a variation of traditional 'one-nation' conservative paternalism, pragmatism and moderation that favoured Keynesian state intervention and welfare.

A3 Margaret Thatcher was elected as leader of the Conservative Party in 1975 and as prime minister in 1979. 'Thatcherism' — New Right neo-liberalism and neo-conservatism — gradually began to emerge thereafter.

***examiner's* note** Before 1979 the UK Conservative Party was traditionalist; thereafter it was Thatcherite.

The UK Conservative Party 1979–2005

Q1 Define 'Thatcherism'.

Q2 Why did Thatcherism emerge in the 1970s?

Q3 Why did the Conservative Party seek to abandon Thatcherism after Margaret Thatcher's resignation in 1990?

ANSWERS

A1 Thatcherism was the UK variant of New Right conservatism. It combined free-market economics, privatisation of public services and cuts in taxation and welfare with authoritarian social, moral and law and order policies.

A2 • Economic recession and 'stagflation' seemed to prove that Keynesian state interventionism had failed.
   • Many Conservatives perceived a growing culture of 'welfare dependency', which they rejected.
   • They also rejected the moral laxity of the 'permissive society' of the 1960s and 1970s.
   • UK membership of the EU since 1973 seemed to threaten national sovereignty and cultural integrity.

A3 The Thatcherite Conservative Party was seen as the 'nasty party': economically uncaring to the poor and also morally illiberal.

examiner's **note** Thatcherism profoundly divided the UK Conservative Party, which has yet to resolve these ideological divisions.

The UK Conservative Party today

Q1 Why was Thatcherism rejected by the UK Conservative Party?

Q2 Why was David Cameron elected as Conservative leader in 2005?

Q3 Summarise the main features of Cameron's conservatism.

ANSWERS

A1 The Conservatives suffered three consecutive general election defeats from 1997 to 2005.

A2 David Cameron — young and media-friendly — wowed the 2005 Conservative conference with a speech without notes.

A3 Cameron's Conservatives began largely as social liberals, combining elements of traditional conservatism with green politics, a belief in social justice, and an internationalist concern for global poverty — but also Euroscepticism. They also sought the inclusion of more young, female and ethnic-minority candidates and members. By 2009, however, there was more — Thatcherite — stress on tax cuts, law and order, family values, anti-immigration and Euroscepticism. There were frequent controversies about party 'sleaze', for example expenses and donations.

***examiner's* note** The Conservative Party is still struggling today to find its ideological base.

Socialism: core doctrines

Q1 What is meant by 'collectivism'?

Q2 Outline the socialist view of human nature.

Q3 Why do socialists believe in equality?

ANSWERS

A1 Collectivism is the belief that humans operate best in cooperative social groups and that such collaborative action for the common good is more efficient and harmonious than selfish, competitive individualism.

A2 Socialists have an optimistic view of human nature as essentially social, cooperative and altruistic — and where it is not, it is the fault of nurture rather than nature, i.e. of the capitalist economic system. Socialists believe that human nature is 'plastic' and can be moulded by circumstance.

A3 Social and economic inequalities are perceived to be much more the result of external economic disadvantages, barriers and injustices than of personal inadequacies.

examiner's **note** When examination questions ask simply about 'socialism', always address both revolutionary and evolutionary socialism — usually in that order.

Utopian socialism

Q1 What is meant by 'utopia'?

Q2 What is meant by 'utopianism'?

Q3 Why is the negative usage of 'utopian' applied to some forms of socialism?

ANSWERS

A1 A 'utopia' is any ideal society, system or way of life.

A2 'Utopianism' — devised by Sir Thomas More in his book *Utopia* (1516) — is a form of theorising about a perfect but non-existent society. The term is usually employed to highlight and criticise the perceived evils of present-day society. The negative usage of 'utopian' implies an idealistic vision of an unattainable fantasy.

A3 Some philosophies, for example conservatism, call socialism 'utopian' in the negative sense because they reject socialism's optimistic view of human nature or because they reject the feasibility of radical socialist goals such as the abolition of capitalism and state.

***examiner's* note** Utopian socialism of the nineteenth century — e.g. Robert Owen and Charles Fourier — is a sub-strand of revolutionary socialism.

Marxism

Q1 What is meant when it is said that Marxism is a 'materialist' theory?

Q2 Explain the Marxist concept of 'exploitation'.

Q3 What did Marx mean by the economic stage he described as the 'dictatorship of the proletariat'?

ANSWERS

A1 A materialist theory sees economic factors as of primary importance.

A2 Exploitation is the extraction of surplus value by the bourgeoisie (the ruling class) from the proletariat (the working class) in the capitalist process of production. This is an inevitable process because it is the only possible source of profit, but it creates a conflict of interests between the bourgeoisie and the proletariat.

A3 The dictatorship of the proletariat is the transitional period of working-class rule immediately after revolution; it is necessary to defend against counter-revolution by the bourgeoisie. When the economy has been collectivised and classes have been abolished, this workers' state will 'wither away'.

***examiner's* note** Marx's theory of 'scientific socialism' was objective, empirical, rational, logical and predictive — unlike 'utopian socialism'.

(33) **ANSWERS**

Parliamentary socialism

Q1 Give two alternative terms for 'parliamentary socialism'.

Q2 Give reasons for the emergence and rise of parliamentary socialism.

Q3 List three forms of parliamentary socialism.

ANSWERS

A1 Parliamentary socialism is also known as 'evolutionary socialism' or 'gradualism'.

A2 It emerged in the late nineteenth and early twentieth centuries as the right to vote was extended to the working class. The nationalism and patriotism of the First and Second World Wars strengthened people's attachment to the state. Rising living standards in Western economies created an increasingly affluent and deradicalised working class — who also increasingly valued the reforms, rights and freedoms already won within Western capitalism, such as trade unionism. Structural changes and technological advances also created a growing middle class.

A3 Democratic socialism, social democracy and New Labour.

***examiner's* note** The goals, as well as the means, of parliamentary socialists are usually more limited and moderate than those of revolutionary socialists.

 ANSWERS

Democratic socialism
versus social democracy

Q1 The concept of 'democratic socialism' has two possible meanings. What are they?

Q2 Explain the significance of 'Clause Four'.

Q3 What is meant by 'revisionism'?

ANSWERS

A1 'Democratic socialism' can mean either all forms of parliamentary socialism or, more narrowly, the radical left-wing, Bennite variant of 'old' Labour.

A2 Clause Four of the Labour Party's founding constitution advocated collective ownership (see Number 38). It was the most symbolic commitment of 'old' Labour to socialism.

A3 'Revisionism' refers to postwar, Keynesian social democracy, which advocated social justice redefined as moderate redistribution and welfare in a mixed, mainly private, economy. It emerged in the postwar economic boom as the working class became more affluent and deradicalised by mass-media socialisation, and as the middle class grew in size.

examiner's **note** Answers to questions on parliamentary socialism should usually be structured — chronologically — from the most to the least radical.

The 'third way'

Q1 When and why did the current usage of the 'third way' concept emerge?

Q2 What is now meant by the 'third way'?

Q3 What are the main themes of the 'third way' philosophy?

ANSWERS

A1 In the 1990s Western developments, such as the decline of the traditional working class and the rise of globalisation, meant that traditional socialism seemed no longer viable, and thus a new concept emerged.

A2 The term 'third way' is used to describe an ideological position somewhere between free-market capitalism and state socialism (or a fusion of the two). It is often labelled 'neo-revisionism'.

A3 • Acceptance of the market over and above the state
   • Emphasis on community and moral responsibility rather than egoistic individualism
   • Pursuit of consensus rather than conflict
   • Belief in social inclusion — 'a hand up, not a hand out'
   • Provision of an enabling state rather than a nanny state

***examiner's* note** A common theme of examination questions is whether or not the 'third way' constitutes a coherent ideological stance.

Comparisons and contrasts within socialism

Q1 What is meant by 'fundamentalist' socialism?

Q2 What is meant by 'revisionist' socialism?

Q3 How does this typology differ from that of 'revolutionary' versus 'evolutionary' socialism?

ANSWERS

A1 Fundamentalist socialism rejects capitalism entirely and seeks to abolish and replace it with socialism in the form of common ownership and substantial equality of outcome.

A2 Revisionist socialism, by contrast, seeks to reform or tame capitalism rather than abolish it. It seeks social justice in the sense of narrowing the economic and social inequalities (to varying degrees) within capitalism through welfare and redistribution. The prime example is postwar social democracy.

A3 The distinction between fundamentalist and revisionist socialism is about ends, whereas the distinction between revolutionary and evolutionary socialism is about means. The founders of the Labour Party were parliamentary fundamentalists.

***examiner's* note** Whether or not New Labour's third way, or even postwar social democracy, are actually socialist is a matter for debate.

(37) ANSWERS

The history of the UK Labour Party

Q1 When and why was the UK Labour Party founded?

Q2 What was the early philosophy of the Labour Party?

Q3 What was Clause Four?

ANSWERS

A1 The UK Labour Party was founded in 1900 as the political agent of the working-class movement in Parliament.

A2 Before the Second World War, radical democratic socialism was the dominant philosophy within the British Labour Party.

A3 Clause Four of Labour's 1918 Constitution read: 'To secure for the workers by hand or by brain the full fruits of their industry and the most equitable distribution thereof that may be possible upon the basis of the common ownership of the means of production, distribution and exchange, and the best obtainable system of popular administration and control of each industry or service.'

examiner's note The history of the UK Labour Party has been characterised by 'revisionism', i.e. a shift from left to right.

The UK Labour Party 1945–95

Q1 When and why did Labour 'revisionism' occur?

Q2 Describe 'social democracy'.

Q3 List four reasons for the emergence of New Labour by 1997.

ANSWERS

A1 A more moderate social democracy emerged after the Second World War, due to both the economic boom and the Cold War.

A2 Social democracy advocates a mixed, predominantly private economy with state intervention, e.g. some redistribution through taxation and welfare. By the 1970s, however, economic recession and 'stagflation' seemed to prove that Keynesian interventionism had failed.

A3 Having lost four successive general elections, the UK Labour Party in the mid-1990s decided to 'modernise' in response to: declining working-class numbers; economic globalisation; the collapse of communism; and the discrediting of 'old-fashioned' socialist ideas after almost 20 years of New Right Conservative governments.

***examiner's* note** The postwar Labour Party was motivated by electoral opportunism to modify or abandon its traditional principles.

The UK Labour Party today

Q1 When and why was New Labour born?

Q2 In what ways has New Labour continued to pursue 'old' Labour values?

Q3 In what ways has New Labour pursued Thatcherite policies?

ANSWERS

A1 The 'new' Labour Party was born in the mid-1990s under the leadership of Tony Blair. For reasons, see Number 39, A3.

A2 • By opting into the EU Social Chapter (e.g. minimum wage)
   • By greatly increasing spending on education and health
   • By setting goals to eradicate child and pensioner poverty

A3 Neo-liberal New Right policies of New Labour:
   • Abolition of the 10p tax band
   • Privatisation of air traffic control, the Tote, the London Tube etc.

   Neo-conservative New Right policies of New Labour:
   • Attempts to extend detention without charge for foreign terror suspects
   • Record prison numbers, CCTV cameras and database records of citizens
   • 'British jobs for British people' (Gordon Brown)

***examiner's* note** Critics have argued that New Labour's 'third way' is incoherent and is guided only by electoral advantage and an obsession with presentation.

40 ANSWERS

Anarchism: core doctrines

Q1 Outline the origins of anarchism.

Q2 Outline the core doctrines of anarchism.

Q3 Summarise the few core doctrines upon which all anarchists agree.

ANSWERS

A1 William Godwin (1756–1836) was perhaps the first anarchistic thinker. Pierre-Joseph Proudhon (1809–65) was the first to announce proudly, in 1840: 'I am an anarchist.' The term derives from the ancient Greek *anarkhia*, meaning, literally, 'no rule'.

A2 Anarchism is a philosophy that rejects all forms of coercion, especially state and government. Anarchists have a highly optimistic view of human nature: 'Perfectibility is the most unequivocal characteristic of the human species' (Godwin).

A3 • Faith in human nature
   • Freedom as a primary goal
   • Opposition to all forms of coercive power, especially state and government
   • Revolutionary transformation of existing society
   • Direct democracy

***examiner's* note** The commonplace and pejorative usage of 'anarchism', to imply chaos and disorder, is not relevant to a philosophical understanding of the concept.

41 ANSWERS

Anarchism and democracy

Q1 Is anarchism anti-democratic?

Q2 Explain the anarchist critique of representative democracy.

Q3 Why do anarchists reject the principle of consent?

ANSWERS

A1 No. Anarchists reject what is commonly called 'representative democracy', because they believe that it is not democratic *enough*.

A2 Representative democracy is neither representative nor democratic, say anarchists. It does not reflect the genuine views or interests of the voters. It is also, of course, associated with state authority, which anarchists reject out of hand. They argue that representative democracy actually entails the surrender of personal sovereignty from the individual to illegitimate governments.

A3 The concept of consent simply perpetuates the myths of government's public accountability and rule in the public interest. It recruits people into colluding with their own oppression by concealing the reality of absolute state power.

***examiner's* note** Anarchists reject all forms of representative democracy equally, whether liberal or totalitarian.

Left- and right-wing anarchism

Q1 Outline the two major strands of anarchist thought.

Q2 Distinguish between left- and right-wing anarchism.

Q3 Describe the two main sub-strands of left-wing anarchism.

Q4 Describe the two main sub-strands of right-wing anarchism.

ANSWERS

A1 Two broad strands of anarchist thought are: collectivist anarchism — ultra-socialism; and individualist anarchism — ultra-liberalism.

A2 The left-wing ultra-socialists are revolutionary, utopian collectivists who have a strong faith in human altruism and seek various forms of egalitarian society. The right-wing ultra-liberals are individualists with a strong faith in human rationality.

A3 'Anarcho-communists' envisage small, egalitarian and self-governing communes that interrelate on the basis of cooperation and communitarianism. 'Anarcho-syndicalists' are more focused upon the collective ownership of industry by the workers.

A4 'Anarcho-capitalists' envisage an absolutely unfettered free market. Max Stirner's 'egoism' perceives each rational and autonomous person to be the centre of his or her own moral universe.

examiner's **note** Left- and right-wing anarchists have profoundly different visions of their ideal, stateless society.

Collectivist anarchism

Q1 Define 'collectivism'.

Q2 Explain the link between collectivism and anarchism.

Q3 What is the main sub-strand of collectivist anarchism?

ANSWERS ▶▶

A1 Collectivism is the belief that cooperative social action is both more ethical and more efficient than is selfish individualism. It is based on the belief that humans are innately social and altruistic creatures.

A2 The logic of this stance is that a peaceful and harmonious society can be achieved naturally and spontaneously through cooperation between social groups, without the need for a coercive state above them; indeed, the state undermines social harmony.

A3 Kropotkin's anarcho-communism employs a form of social Darwinism to argue that humans have been able to evolve and advance because of cooperation, not competition.

***examiner's* note** Collectivist anarchism is the most optimistic of all philosophies in its faith in the human capacity for cooperation.

Anarchism versus Marxism

Q1 Left-wing anarchism and Marxism are two different forms of revolutionary socialism. Explain.

Q2 How does Marxist 'materialist' theory differ from anarchism?

Q3 Summarise the main philosophical differences between Marxism and anarchism.

ANSWERS

A1 Collectivist anarchism is 'utopian socialism' — idealist, emotive and moralising — whereas Marxism is 'scientific socialism' — empirical, objective and determinist.

A2 Marxism focuses primarily on the economic infrastructure. The state is merely the political agent of the economic ruling class. For anarchists, on the other hand, the state is the primary target of attack.

A3

Marxism		Anarchism
Materialist theory		Political theory
Scientific socialism		Utopian socialism
State is mere superstructure		State is primary target
Explains state	versus	Condemns state
Endorses proletarian state		Rejects any state
State will wither away		State must be overthrown

examiner's note Collectivist anarchists such as Bakunin argued that Marx was naive in thinking that the state would simply 'wither away' after revolution. The state must be overthrown.

45 ANSWERS

Individualist anarchism

Q1 Define 'individualism'.

Q2 Explain the link between individualism and anarchism.

Q3 What is the main sub-strand of individualist anarchism?

ANSWERS

A1 Individualism is the belief in the primacy of the individual, and his or her autonomy, rights and freedoms over any group, society or state.

A2 Individualist anarchism views human nature as rational and self-striving, and therefore as deserving of freedom from any coercion and control, especially from state and government.

A3 The main sub-strand of individualist anarchism is anarcho-capitalism, an extreme form of classical *laissez faire*: that is, private police and courts, no compulsory taxation or education, no welfare state, no state regulation of health and safety at work or of the content of foods or medicines etc.

***examiner's* note** Individualist anarchism is clearly rooted in early forms of liberalism, which it has taken to its furthest possible conclusion. It is only its extreme antipathy towards the state that has earned it the label 'anarchist'.

Anarchism versus liberalism

Q1 Outline the major difference between anarchism and liberalism.

Q2 Outline another difference between anarchism and liberalism.

Q3 Summarise the main philosophical differences between liberalism and anarchism.

ANSWERS

A1 All liberals perceive that the state can act to protect individuals' freedoms. Even classical liberals perceived the state as a 'necessary evil' and advocated a 'nightwatchman state' to ensure order. Modern liberals favour a much more interventionist state to enhance positive freedom. Anarchists, however, see the state as an 'unnecessary evil' — irredeemably oppressive and corrupting.

A2 All anarchists are revolutionary, whereas liberals are, at most, reformist.

A3

Liberalism		Anarchism
State is necessary evil (classical)		State is unnecessary evil
State aids positive freedom (modern)		State negates freedom
Favours constitutionalism and consent	versus	Believes constitutionalism and consent are sham
'Rule of law' protects liberty		All law infringes liberty
Reformist		Revolutionary

***examiner's* note** Anarchists and liberals have different concepts of freedom, deriving from different views of the state.

Anarchist strategies and tactics

Q1 Are anarchists advocates of peaceful or violent tactics?

Q2 On what grounds have some anarchists advocated violent tactics?

Q3 What political methods are, logically, not utilised by anarchists?

ANSWERS

A1 Anarchism was originally — and logically — pacifist. Since anarchists reject coercion in all its forms, and since violence is the ultimate form of coercion, most anarchists naturally reject it. Some anarchists, however, have turned to violence.

A2 Sheer frustration at their lack of success, a belief in the nihilistic virtue of destruction, the need to counter a violent state or simply the desire to expose the inherently violent nature of the state by provoking it.

A3 What anarchists philosophically cannot do is participate in mainstream, orthodox, ballot-box and party politics, since that would be subscribing to the politics of the state.

***examiner's* note** Part of anarchism's continuing appeal is its rejection of mainstream politics.

Anarchism: some problems

Q1 Why may anarchism be viewed as 'utopian' in both a positive and a negative sense?

Q2 Why may different schools of anarchist thought be viewed as more or less utopian?

Q3 In what sense is anarchism strong on moral principle but weak on explanation?

ANSWERS

A1 Utopians envisage a perfect future society of peace, freedom and harmony. Anarchists would happily accept this label, believing that their goal of a stateless yet harmonious society is entirely achievable. In the negative sense, a utopian is one who seeks an impossibly idealised society. Most mainstream political philosophies label anarchism as utopian in this negative sense.

A2 Left-wing anarchists have the most optimistic belief in human perfectibility and collectivism, whereas individualist anarchists are simply taking contemporary free-market ideology to its logical conclusion.

A3 Anarchism is good at condemning the state but weak on explaining the state, its origins and its enduring authority.

examiner's note Despite criticism, anarchism flourishes because it is the most optimistic and uplifting belief in human betterment yet devised.

Anarchism and utopia

Q1 Explain the link between anarchism and the positive usage of 'utopian'.

Q2 Why do conservatives label anarchism as 'utopian' in a negative sense?

Q3 Why do Marxists label anarchism as 'utopian' in a negative sense?

ANSWERS

A1 Utopian theories envisage a perfect future society of peace, freedom and harmony, which is attainable because human nature is inherently rational or altruistic — a positive interpretation that anarchists would proudly accept. They stress that, until some 6,000 years ago, all humans lived in stateless societies. Anarchist thinking is grounded as much in strong faith in social structures — such as common ownership or the free market — as in faith in human nature.

A2 Conservatives view the anarchist conception of human nature as over-optimistic (see Number 21).

A3 Marxists argue that anarchists lack scientific analysis of the economic roots of social conflict and therefore lack adequate strategies for social transformation.

***examiner's* note** Whether anarchism is labelled utopian depends, crucially, upon the definition of 'utopian' employed.

Nation versus state

Q1 Distinguish between a 'nation' and a 'state'.

Q2 Why do so many nations seek statehood?

Q3 Why are many states not nation-states?

ANSWERS ▶▶

A1 A 'nation' is a group of people with a shared sense of common cultural heritage, whereas a 'state' is a sovereign, political power over a given territory.

A2 Most nationalist movements desire statehood for self-determination and political autonomy, domestic unity and cohesion and international peace and order.

A3 Most states are multicultural, for example the UK, which comprises, at least, the English, Scottish, Welsh and Northern Irish nations. Also, a nation may be dispersed across many states — e.g. the Jews before the creation of Israel in 1948. Many nations today still seek a state, for example the Palestinians or Kurds.

***examiner's* note** A 'nation' is a much more subjective identity, i.e. a matter of sentiment and self-identity, than is a 'state'.

Liberal nationalism

Q1 When did nationalism first emerge?

Q2 In what ways is nationalism compatible with liberalism?

Q3 In what ways does nationalism conflict with liberalism?

ANSWERS ▶▶

A1 Liberal nationalism was the earliest form of nationalism. It was associated with the French Revolution and Enlightenment era.

A2 Liberal nationalism regards nations in the same way as liberal theory regards individuals: that is, they are moral entities deserving of freedom, autonomy and self-determination. The liberal belief in balance and harmony is also reflected in the liberal nationalist idea that a world of independent nation-states will be peaceful and stable. Liberal nationalism is peaceful, constitutional and reformist.

A3 Some liberal writers, such as Elie Kedourie (*Nationalism*, 1974), dislike the collectivist and emotional nature of nationalism, as well as its tendency to regression, exclusion, intolerance, violence and even racism and dictatorship.

***examiner's* note** Many examination questions focus on liberalism's ambivalence towards nationalism.

Conservative nationalism

Q1 Why do organic conservatives value nationalism?

Q2 Why have conservatives feared cultural diversity?

Q3 What forms of nationalism do conservatives reject?

ANSWERS ▶▶

A1 Conservatism regards cultural unity, patriotism and an emotional attachment to the traditional symbols of the state — such as the flag and the monarchy — as sources of social stability and organic cohesion. The organic principles of continuity and consensus are epitomised by a belief in national heritage and national unity.

A2 Conservatism fears cultural diversity because of its view of human beings as psychologically imperfect and in need of a sense of security and common identity. Cultural diversity generates rootlessness, personal insecurity, conflict and even social breakdown.

A3 Conservatives reject forms of nationalism that are radical or revolutionary (see Numbers 54–55).

***examiner's* note** Conservative nationalism can range from benevolent paternalism to authoritarian intolerance.

 (53) ANSWERS

Chauvinist nationalism

Q1 Define 'chauvinist nationalism'.

Q2 Why is chauvinist nationalism so called?

Q3 Give three examples of chauvinist nationalism.

ANSWERS

A1 Chauvinist nationalism is expansionist, aggressive, militaristic and ethnocentric. That is, embodying a sense not only of cultural distinction, but also of inherent cultural superiority, justifying the nation's right to impose its control and culture upon other 'inferior' nations and states through war and conquest.

A2 Chauvinist nationalism was named after the French Napoleonic soldier Nicolas Chauvin, whose fervent nationalism spawned the derogatory label of 'chauvinism' in a nineteenth-century France that had lost its nationalist zeal.

A3 Examples of chauvinist nationalism include: nineteenth-century British imperialism when the European states engaged in a 'scramble for Africa'; Italian fascism (see Number 64); and Serbia in the 1990s.

***examiner's* note** Chauvinist nationalism is the form of nationalism most vehemently rejected by liberal nationalists.

Anti-colonial nationalism

Q1 When and why did anti-colonial nationalism emerge?

Q2 In what ways is nationalism compatible with communism?

Q3 In what ways does nationalism conflict with communism?

ANSWERS ▶▶

A1 Anti-colonial nationalism (often communist) emerged in the second half of the twentieth century, mainly in less developed countries seeking freedom from imperial rule. For example, India gained independence from the British Empire in 1947.

A2 Communism and nationalism combine well in practice to generate a popular, collectivist movement against foreign oppressors who are both capitalist and imperialist.

A3 Since communist theory is internationalist ('Working men of all countries, unite!' wrote Marx), communist forms of nationalism are inherently contradictory in theory.

***examiner's* note** Anti-colonial nationalism embodies many paradoxes of nationalism itself: it may be peaceful or violent, democratic or dictatorial and it is described as 'Janus-like', after the two-headed god, because it looks both backwards to history and forwards to modernisation.

Political and cultural nationalism

Q1 What is 'political nationalism'?

Q2 What is 'cultural nationalism'?

Q3 Give examples to illustrate the differences between the two concepts.

ANSWERS

A1 'Political nationalism' is defined by the principle of self-determination, whether expressed in the desire for some measure of autonomy in the form of devolution or federalism, or in the fully developed form of sovereign statehood.

A2 'Cultural nationalism' is associated with the defence of a nation's cultural heritage, without any strong desire for political autonomy.

A3 Political nationalism may be liberal (e.g. the Scottish National Party), communist (e.g. Cuba) or chauvinist, i.e. expansionist and aggressive (e.g. Italian fascism). An example of cultural nationalism is the Welsh desire to protect and promote Wales's distinctive language. It often leans to conservatism.

***examiner's* note** Political and cultural nationalism are sub-types within and across the four main types of nationalism described in Numbers 52–55.

Racism

Q1 What is 'racism'?

Q2 In what circumstances does racism tend to emerge?

Q3 Explain the link between racism and imperialism.

ANSWERS ▶▶

A1 Racism/racialism is the perception that humans can be categorised meaningfully into ethnic or biological castes, and that these groups can be ranked in a hierarchy that has economic, political, social and/or psychological significance.

A2 Racism tends to emerge in times of economic downturn when people feel insecure, threatened and resentful, and seek scapegoats for their social ills.

A3 The nineteenth and early twentieth centuries were characterised by capitalist imperialism, where European states rationalised their conquest of African countries with reference to 'the white man's burden', as the British poet Rudyard Kipling put it — the assertion that superior whites had a missionary duty to civilise the blacks.

***examiner's* note** Racism is often justified by reference to pseudo-scientific theories of 'social Darwinism'.

57 ANSWERS

Nationalism and racism

Q1 What is the main difference between nationalism and racism?

Q2 Outline other key differences between the two concepts.

Q3 Why are the two concepts often confused?

ANSWERS

A1 Nations are cultural entities, whereas races are genetically defined.

A2

Nationalism		Racism
Culture		Biology
No necessary assertion of hierarchy		Definite assertion of hierarchy
Territorial claims	versus	No necessary territorial claims
Left, centre or right wing		Right wing
Rational or irrational		Irrational

A3 The two terms are often confused, or used interchangeably, especially by right-wing nationalists who define nationhood in terms of ethnicity — an exclusive perspective usually designed to legitimise hierarchy, separation or other forms of oppression. Conservative nationalism sometimes leans to this perspective, but it is explicit in the ethnic nationalism of Nazism, and the BNP.

examiner's note Nationalism is much more flexible and adaptable, and therefore more prevalent, than is racism. The two doctrines may overlap, however, both in theory and in practice.

Forms of nationalism in the UK

Q1 Describe the form of nationalism in Scotland.

Q2 Describe the form of nationalism in Wales.

Q3 Describe the forms of nationalism in Northern Ireland.

Q4 Describe the form of nationalism in England.

ANSWERS

A1 Scottish nationalists exhibit a political form of liberal nationalism in their desire for some measure of autonomy.

A2 Welsh nationalists seek to defend and promote their nation's cultural heritage, particularly their distinctive language.

A3 In Northern Ireland, the Republicans pursue an agenda of anti-colonial nationalism against the English conquerors and settlers. The Unionists are, essentially, conservative UK nationalists.

A4 English nationalism is defensive and often exclusive, wary of alien cultures and races. It leans to ethnocentrism — a sense of cultural superiority (in part, a heritage of empire) and, therefore, may even take the form of ethnic nationalism or racism.

examiner's **note** The different forms and strengths of nationalism throughout the UK have prompted different types and degrees of devolution.

Beyond nationalism

Q1 Which political ideology wholly rejects nationalism, and why?

Q2 Why does Marxism largely reject nationalism?

Q3 Why is liberalism also wary of nationalism?

ANSWERS

A1 Probably the only philosophy that cannot absorb nationalism is anarchism, since the latter is so fundamentally hostile to any concept of statehood, which is usually the prime goal of nationalist movements.

A2 Marxist theory argues that conflicting class interests divide nations and that working-class consciousness should be internationalist.

A3 Some liberal writers, such as Elie Kedourie (*Nationalism*, 1974), reject the collectivist and emotional nature of nationalism, as well as its tendency to regression, exclusion, intolerance, violence and even racism and dictatorship. They oppose chauvinist nationalism the most strongly.

***examiner's* note** Notwithstanding competing ideologies and contemporary trends such as globalisation, supranationalism, regionalism and localism, nationalism remains one of the most powerful and also paradoxical of all political ideologies.

The origins of fascism

Q1 Briefly define 'fascism'.

Q2 Outline the economic and political circumstances that gave rise to fascism in the 1920s.

Q3 Outline some of the 'negations' of fascism.

ANSWERS

A1 Fascism was an interwar movement that sought to combine absolutist political power and economic regulation with an emotional appeal to national regeneration and glory.

A2 Fascism was generated by: the military humiliation of the First World War; serious economic depression combined with inflation; political instability and alienation. These factors led people to seek strong leadership, security and restored national pride.

A3 Fascism had a very negative nature. It was:
- anti-enlightenment
- anti-rational
- anti-liberal
- anti-individualist
- anti-communist
- anti-egalitarian

***examiner's* note** The exact nature of fascism differed from country to country across Europe.

Anti-rationalism

Q1 What is meant by 'anti-rationalism'?

Q2 How was anti-rationalism manifested within fascism?

Q3 Give one quotation to illustrate fascist anti-rationalism.

ANSWERS

A1 Anti-rationalism embraces a highly negative view of human nature: the idea that humans are motivated not by rational calculation, but by powerful, instinctive and emotional drives and urges.

A2 Fascist theories constituted political myths that sought to stimulate political activism by appealing, through powerful symbols, to the emotions and instincts of the masses. Fascist anti-intellectualism was also reflected in a stress upon physical prowess, reflected in a glorification of the body and the 'life-force' or a stress upon might and military power.

A3 Mussolini said, 'Think with your blood.'

***examiner's* note** 'Anti-rationalism' — a view of human nature — should not be confused with 'irrationalism' — the assertion that fascist policies were simply not logical or sensible.

Fascism: core doctrines

Q1 Outline the fascist view of state and society.

Q2 Outline the fascist view of leadership.

Q3 Was fascism nationalist or racist?

ANSWERS

A1 Fascism centred upon a supremely organic view of the state and hence a collectivist, but highly elitist and anti-egalitarian, view of society.

A2 Fascism — especially Nazism — epitomised the 'leader principle': the belief in a single, all-powerful, charismatic leader who embodied the 'will of the people' and, therefore, could not err.

A3 Italian fascism was overwhelmingly nationalist — for Mussolini, it was enough to be Italian. German Nazism, however, was overwhelmingly racist and sought to eliminate 'inferior biological species' such as Jews, blacks, homosexuals, gypsies and the disabled.

***examiner's* note** Fascist movements embraced an incoherent and irrational set of values centring on the state and leader, nationalism or racism and myths of 'Darwinian' struggle that extolled war, violence, power and action.

Italian fascism

Q1 When did Italian fascism (led by Benito Mussolini) come to power?

Q2 What was the key doctrine of Italian fascism?

Q3 What kind of nationalism was practised by Italian fascism?

ANSWERS

A1 1922.

A2 Italian fascist theory centred on the primacy of the supremely
organic state as 'the march of God upon the Earth' (Hegel), with
the leader — *Il Duce* — in theory the servant of the state. As the
fascist ideologue Giovanni Gentile put it: 'Everything for the state;
nothing against the state; nothing outside the state.' Italian fascism
devised the concept of the 'totalitarian state' based on mass
consent and legitimacy and seeking total control of every sphere
of life, the private as well as the public.

A3 Italian fascism embraced a reactionary, ethnocentric and
militaristic form of chauvinist — expansionist — nationalism.

***examiner's* note** All doctrines of Italian fascism centred on the primacy of the
state.

Fascist nationalism

Q1 Define 'chauvinist nationalism'.

Q2 In what sense was fascist nationalism 'reactionary'?

Q3 What was the fascist attitude to war and violence?

ANSWERS

A1 Chauvinist nationalism is expansionist, aggressive and militaristic, with a powerful belief in the superiority of its own culture — ethnocentrism — which justified the state's right to impose its control and culture upon other states through war and conquest.

A2 'Reactionary' means seeking to turn the clock back to an earlier, 'better' time. Italian fascism sought to recreate the glories of the ancient Roman empire.

A3 Fascism glorified war and violence, not just as means but as ends in themselves, as forces for supremacy and purity: 'War is like a cleansing wind across a stagnant sea' (Hegel); or 'War is to men what maternity is to women' (Mussolini).

***examiner's* note** Fascist nationalism links with its anti-rationalism and social Darwinism.

German Nazism

Q1 When did German Nazism (led by Adolph Hitler) come to power?

Q2 What was the key doctrine of German Nazism?

Q3 Did Nazism share Italian fascism's totalitarian aims?

ANSWERS

A1 1933.

A2 Nazi theory asserted the primacy of the leader over everything else, including the state. The Führer was the embodiment of the 'will of the people [*Volk*]' (a perversion of Rousseau's idea of the 'general will' combined with Nietzsche's 'superman'). This did not mean that the Führer followed the will of the people, but that he was the only person capable of interpreting the collective will correctly. This meant that he was infallible. This was also fascism's main philosophical claim to democracy.

A3 The German *Volksstaat* (people's state) rarely employed the concept or theory of totalitarianism, but was arguably more totalitarian in practice than was Italian fascism.

***examiner's* note** Nazism was the most efficient, cruel and ruthless of all the European fascist regimes.

Nazi racism

Q1 Describe the main features of Nazi racial theory.

Q2 What was the goal of Nazi expansionism?

Q3 Where did these racist ideas originate?

ANSWERS

A1 Nazism divided human society into a hierarchy of perceived biological or genetic castes, headed by the culture-creating Aryan master race (*Herrenvolk*). The intermediate, culture-carrying races were to be servants of the master race; and the most inferior, culture-destroying races — Jews, blacks, homosexuals, gypsies, Communists, physically and mentally handicapped (even if they were German) — were to be eliminated.

A2 German expansionism had *Lebensraum* as its goal — living space for the master race. For Nazism, unlike Italian fascism, the race had priority over the state.

A3 This racial theory was not devised by Hitler but was adopted from nineteenth-century ideologists such as Gobineau, Wagner and Chamberlain.

***examiner's* note** Racism is not a core feature of all fascist ideologies.

67 **ANSWERS**

Fascism and Nazism:
contrasts

Q1 Outline two key contrasts between Italian fascism and German Nazism.

Q2 Summarise the main differences between fascism and Nazism.

ANSWERS

A1 Nazism was not primarily nationalist but, instead, overwhelmingly racist. For Nazism, unlike Italian fascism, the race had priority over the state, which was viewed simply as *Lebensraum* — living space for the expanding race. Whereas Italian fascism asserted the primacy of the state, Nazism asserted the primacy of the leader — the *Führerprinzip*. His authority derived not from election, but from charisma and 'natural selection'.

A2

Italian fascism		German Nazism
Primacy of state		Primacy of leader
Nationalist		Racist
Totalitarian theory		Totalitarian practice
Corporate state	versus	State-regulated capitalism
Compromise with Catholic Church and monarchy		Persecution of Church
		More efficient in practice in both coercion and 'consent'

***examiner's* note** Examination questions sometimes ask whether the similarities between fascism and Nazism are greater than the differences.

Fascist claims to democracy

Q1 Explain fascism's main philosophical claim to 'democracy'.

Q2 What kind of authority was exercised by fascist leaders?

Q3 Why did fascism reject liberal democracy?

ANSWERS

A1 Fascism's theoretical claims to democracy were based, above all, on the 'leadership principle', which claimed that the supreme, infallible and all-knowing leader embodied the 'will of the people' and could not err. Fascists believed that the masses were suited only to obeying and following, so their consent was unnecessary. Thus the absolute dictatorship of the leader with a monopoly of ideological wisdom was the only true form of democracy.

A2 Fascist leaders possessed mainly charismatic authority — based on magnetic personality — but combined with elements of traditional, and sometimes legal-rational, authority.

A3 Fascists despised the division and diversity of liberal democracy and, instead, embraced 'totalitarian democracy' and 'strength through unity'.

***examiner's* note** Fascist 'totalitarian democracy' was the antithesis of liberal democracy.

Fascism and socialism/communism

Q1 Outline the main similarities between fascism and socialism.

Q2 Outline the main differences between fascism and socialism.

Q3 What was the fascist attitude to private property?

ANSWERS

A1 Fascism does have a strongly collectivist and communitarian aspect to it as it places society and the nation above individuals.

A2

Fascism/Nazism		Socialism/communism
Right wing		Left wing
Negative view of human nature		Positive view of human nature
Organic, elitist collectivism		Egalitarian collectivism
Nationalist/racist		Internationalist
National/racial Darwinism	versus	Economic Darwinism
War and national/racial conflict		Economic/class conflict
Eternal conflict		Ultimate peace and harmony
Pro state-regulated capitalism		Anti private property
Totalitarian state		'Withering away' of the state

A3 Fascism was an extreme right-wing movement, stressing private property and hierarchy. It was funded and supported by the business classes, who prospered by it.

***examiner's* note** As the historian Hugh Trevor-Roper put it, 'Before all else, fascism was anti-communist. It lived and throve on anti-communism.'

The origins of multiculturalism

Q1 Define 'culture'.

Q2 What is meant by 'multiculturalism' as a political concept?

Q3 When did the term gain political currency?

ANSWERS

A1 According to the Oxford English Dictionary, a 'culture' is 'the customs, civilization and achievements of a particular time or people'.

A2 As a political viewpoint, 'multiculturalism' implies approval of cultural diversity within a society as a catalyst for self-worth, mutual tolerance, social vibrancy and broader social unity — 'diversity within unity' (Andrew Heywood, *Political Ideologies*, 2007).

A3 The term only became commonplace in political debate in the 1990s, although it first emerged as an ideological viewpoint in the 1960s US black consciousness movement. The term 'multiculturalism' was first used in Canada in 1965 to describe an accepting and encouraging approach to bilingualism within that country.

***examiner's* note** Multiculturalism refers to national, religious or racial differences rather than class, geographic or demographic distinctions.

 71 ANSWERS

Multiculturalism: usages

Q1 Give one descriptive usage of the concept of multiculturalism.

Q2 Give one ideological usage of the concept of multiculturalism.

Q3 Give one political usage of the concept of multiculturalism.

ANSWERS

A1 'Multiculturalism' can be simply a descriptive term for racial, ethnic, cultural and linguistic diversities within a society.

A2 'Multiculturalism' can be a normative term for the positive endorsement of cultural diversity, recognition of the rights of diverse groups and celebration of the benefits to society that such diversity brings. This is its political, or 'ideological', usage. It is associated primarily with liberal thinking.

A3 'Multiculturalism' can refer to government endorsements of cultural diversity, for example the political accommodation of post-immigration minorities, either in public policy or institutional structures (which may involve 'consociationalism' — power-sharing structures between diverse cultural communities, e.g. in Switzerland, Belgium and Northern Ireland).

examiner's **note** Multiculturalism is a quite new and contested concept in modern politics.

Multiculturalism: features

Q1 What factors have enhanced cultural diversity since the Second World War?

Q2 Multiculturalism embraces 'identity politics'. Explain this concept.

Q3 Why does multiculturalism favour diversity?

ANSWERS

A1   There were substantial increases in migration, globalisation and 'post-colonialism' after 1945, which sought to challenge Eurocentrism and the cultural hegemony of Western imperial ideas and assumptions, and reject the universalist pretensions of Western liberal ideology. One example was Gandhi's Indian nationalism.

A2   Identity politics perceives people in terms of their cultural characteristics and stresses the importance of factors such as language, religion and ethnicity in shaping personal and social identity.

A3   Diversity is the belief that cultural differences are compatible with citizenship and social/political cohesion. Whereas nationalists believe largely that citizenship should be based on cultural homogeneity, multiculturalism believes that a denial of cultural diversity may generate resentment, isolation and extremism.

***examiner's* note** Some philosophies, such as conservatism, dislike cultural diversity (see Number 53).

(73) **ANSWERS**

Minority rights

Q1 Explain the concept of minority rights, embraced by multiculturalism.

Q2 Why do multiculturalists defend minority rights?

Q3 Why are minority rights controversial?

ANSWERS ▶▶

A1 Minority rights are the entitlements of a particular group to representation, self-government and legal protections (e.g. of dress codes or religious holidays). In education, work or political representation they often include reverse or 'positive' discrimination (termed 'affirmative action' in the USA).

A2 Minority rights help to protect cultural and hence personal identity, and they help to redress under-representation and negative discrimination or disadvantage.

A3 Minority rights may hamper cultural integration (e.g. the issue of the veil for Muslim women); they may be seen as unfair or counterproductive, especially if they entail positive discrimination; and they may conflict with liberal notions of freedom of expression.

examiner's **note** There are inevitable tensions between minority group rights, majority rights and individual rights. These pose dilemmas for liberal thinking.

Liberal multiculturalism

Q1 Explain the concept of liberal multiculturalism.

Q2 Are there limits to liberal tolerance of cultural differences?

Q3 Suggest one ideological dilemma faced by liberal multiculturalists.

ANSWERS

A1 Liberal multiculturalism embodies a belief in individual freedom to cherish and celebrate one's distinctive cultural identity and, above all, in tolerance of cultural differences and disagreements. This reflects liberal beliefs in human rationalism, freedom of choice in the moral sphere and the view that truth prevails in a free market of ideas.

A2 Liberal tolerance is not morally neutral; it only extends to cultures that are, themselves, tolerant and rights-orientated; it may not extend, for example, to female circumcision or forced marriages.

A3 The liberal belief in individual rights conflicts with multiculturalism's emphasis on group rights.

examiner's **note** Liberal multiculturalism requires a liberal democratic framework and may not support other political systems, such as an Islamic state based on *sharia* law.

Pluralist multiculturalism

Q1 Explain the concept of pluralist multiculturalism.

Q2 Why would liberals reject pluralist multiculturalism?

Q3 Suggest one further criticism of pluralist multiculturalism.

ANSWERS

A1 Pluralist multiculturalism goes further than liberal multiculturalism in accepting the equal validity and legitimacy of liberal, non-liberal and illiberal ideas and values, even though they may be incompatible or even incomparable — i.e. moral pluralism.

A2 For liberals, pluralist multiculturalism poses the dilemma of how far to tolerate intolerant or oppressive beliefs. Moral pluralism may also be premised on moral indifference, which may be dangerous.

A3 Pluralist multiculturalism may undermine civic cohesion and social unity, especially where it takes the 'particularist' form of defending or even prioritising the identities and interests of groups perceived as oppressed or corrupted by decadent, colonial and racist Western culture.

***examiner's* note** Pluralist multiculturalism implies a 'post-liberal' stance, where liberal ideas and values can no longer claim moral supremacy.

Cosmopolitan multiculturalism

Q1 Explain the concept of cosmopolitan multiculturalism.

Q2 Explain the inherent paradox in this view of multiculturalism.

Q3 Suggest one further problem for cosmopolitan multiculturalists.

ANSWERS

A1 Cosmopolitan multiculturalism values cultural diversity in so far as different cultures can share and learn from each other, as a transitional step on the way to international identity and harmony, or a world state.

A2 Cosmopolitanism and multiculturalism are essentially conflicting ideas, because cosmopolitanism believes in international or global identity transcending particular cultures. It perceives society as a melting-pot of different values and lifestyles — 'hybridity' — which may fundamentally blur and weaken distinctive cultural identities.

A3 Cosmopolitanism is not a widespread perspective in a world where powerful localist, nationalist and even racist sentiments still pervade.

***examiner's* note** Multiculturalism is often a reaction against globalisation and the subsequent merging — or submerging — of national identities.

77 ANSWERS

Critical perspectives on multiculturalism

Q1 Outline a conservative critique of multiculturalism.

Q2 Outline a socialist critique of multiculturalism.

Q3 Outline a feminist critique of multiculturalism.

ANSWERS

A1 Conservatives believe that security-seeking individuals and a stable society require cultural homogeneity. Multiculturalism is therefore a threat to social cohesion and majority interests, and 'diversity within unity' is a myth.

A2 Socialists argue that it is not a lack of cultural recognition that encumbers some groups, but rather their lack of economic power and social status. Multiculturalism is a form of 'divide and rule' of oppressed and exploited classes, which may distract or detract from redistributive and welfare politics.

A3 Feminists object specifically to patriarchal cultures that legitimise and perpetuate the oppression of women in their power structures, family arrangements, moral or dress codes. Hence they object to multicultural perspectives that defend such cultures.

***examiner's* note** Even liberal individualism conflicts essentially with multicultural collectivism and communitarianism.

Multiculturalism in the UK

Q1 How recent is multiculturalism in the UK?

Q2 How may incidents of racial aggression and terrorism in the UK be interpreted by critics of multiculturalism?

Q3 How may incidents of racial aggression and terrorism in the UK be interpreted by advocates of multiculturalism?

ANSWERS

A1 The UK has long been a multicultural society, comprising — at least — the English, Scots, Welsh and Irish. In the last decade, however, 'multicultural' has come to be equated with 'multiethnic' and 'multiracial'.

A2 Such incidents are seen as the consequence of misguided multiculturalism and as shattering the implicit social consensus that underpins multiculturalism.

A3 For advocates of multiculturalism, such events are the products of cultural repression and can only be assuaged or allayed by accepting and encouraging cultural diversity within the UK.

examiner's **note** New Labour argued that multiculturalism was compatible with Britishness — diversity within unity — and sought to promote both. Critics, however, perceive multiculturalism — as a 'third way' between assimilation and separatism — as an untenable contradiction.

Multiculturalism: a coherent ideology?

Q1 Is multiculturalism essentially a liberal idea?

Q2 Suggest a reason why multiculturalism may lack ideological coherence.

Q3 Which alternative ideologies challenge multiculturalism in the twenty-first century?

ANSWERS

A1 At first sight, multiculturalism seems an eminently liberal concept, redolent of toleration and diversity. There are, however, clear tensions between the communitarian and often particularist facets of multiculturalism and the individualist and universalist traits of liberal theory.

A2 Multiculturalism takes different forms — liberal, pluralist and cosmopolitan — which profoundly challenge and criticise each other.

A3 Nationalism, racism, religious fundamentalism, globalisation and genuine cosmopolitanism will all continue to challenge multiculturalism from different directions — not to mention the critical perspectives outlined in Number 78.

***examiner's* note** Multiculturalism may lack the ideological strength, clarity and coherence of the more enduring and mainstream political philosophies. It also poses a fundamental challenge to all three dominant Western ideologies — liberalism, socialism and especially conservatism.

'First-wave' feminism

Q1 What is feminism, and when did it originate?

Q2 What was 'first-wave' feminism?

Q3 When did women gain the right to vote in the UK?

ANSWERS

A1 Feminism is a philosophy that advocates — at least — equality of rights between the sexes. It was originally an eighteenth- and nineteenth-century movement of middle-class women seeking the vote.

A2 'First-wave' feminism emerged with Mary Wollstonecraft's *Vindication of the Rights of Women* (1792). It sought to reduce sexual discrimination, primarily through a campaign for equal suffrage. It was premised upon the liberal assumption that all individuals — men and women — are rational beings, equally deserving of rights and opportunities.

A3 Women over the age of 30 gained the right to vote in 1918, thanks to the active economic role played by women during the First World War.

***examiner's* note** The suffragettes are probably the best-known example of first-wave feminism.

'Second-wave' feminism

Q1 When and why did 'second-wave' feminism emerge?

Q2 How did second-wave feminism differ from first-wave feminism?

Q3 List the three main schools of second-wave feminism.

ANSWERS

A1 By the 1960s it became increasingly clear that the granting of equal formal political and legal rights had not eliminated widespread and systematic patterns of sexual inequality.

A2 Second-wave feminism was much more diverse and wide-ranging than first-wave feminism, embracing not just liberal ideas, but more radical and even revolutionary schools of feminist thought. It went beyond demands for equality in the public spheres of the workplace, politics and law to challenge long-standing assumptions about women's personal, family, cultural, gender and even biological roles.

A3 The three main schools of second-wave feminism are liberal feminism, socialist feminism and radical feminism.

***examiner's* note** The label 'Women's Liberation Movement' sought to highlight the far-reaching aims of second-wave feminism.

Liberal feminism

Q1 Summarise the main aims of liberal feminism.

Q2 How far does liberal feminism extend in its aims?

Q3 Name one liberal feminist.

ANSWERS

A1 Liberal feminism seeks equal formal rights and more genuine equal opportunities for women through legislative reform. This school of thought seeks changes only in the 'public' sphere of work, politics, education and law, and is reformist in outlook.

A2 Crucially, liberal feminism does not seek to challenge traditional gender roles in the private sphere of home and family, believing these to be a matter of individual choice.

A3 Betty Freidan's book *The Feminist Mystique* (1963) marked the resurgence of feminist thinking in the 1960s.

***examiner's* note** Liberal feminism in the UK achieved reforms such as the Abortion Act (1967), Equal Pay Act (1970), Sex Discrimination Act (1976), the liberalisation of divorce, taxation and property laws, and free contraception.

Socialist feminism

Q1 Summarise the main arguments of socialist feminism.

Q2 How do traditional gender roles benefit capitalism?

Q3 Name one socialist feminist.

ANSWERS

A1 Socialist/Marxist feminism argues that sexual divisions in capitalism are due primarily to the operation of the economy. A class revolution is therefore the prerequisite of sexual equality in the 'public' sphere of the economy, which will, in turn, transform the 'private' sphere of home and family.

A2 The traditional nuclear family provides capitalism with 'two for the price of one' (i.e. male breadwinner and female worker at home, for the price of one wage), also providing men with an incentive to remain in exploitative work to support their families.

A3 Marx's collaborator Friedrich Engels in his book *The Origins of the Family, Private Property and the State* (1884).

examiner's note Marxist feminists emphasise the role of ideology and socialisation in perpetuating gender inequalities and women's acceptance of them.

Radical feminism

Q1 Summarise the key views of radical feminism.

Q2 What is unique about radical feminism?

Q3 Name one radical feminist.

ANSWERS ▶▶

A1 Radical feminism sees the oppression of women as the first, most universal and still pervasive social division. It is a new and revolutionary theory, which challenges all previous political ideologies in being wholly female-centred. It rejects the divide between 'public man' and 'private woman'. It argues that a transformation of relationships in the 'private' sphere of home and family is the prerequisite of wider social equality.

A2 Radical feminism argues that, because of their shared experiences of oppression, all women are united in a common 'sisterhood'.

A3 Writers such as Kate Millett and Shulamith Firestone are radical feminists.

examiner's **note** There are substantial philosophical divisions within radical feminism itself. The most radical of the radicals advocate lesbian separatism or female 'supremacism'.

85 ANSWERS

Patriarchy

Q1 Explain how radical feminists employ the concept of 'patriarchy'.

Q2 What conclusions do radical feminists draw from their analysis of patriarchy?

Q3 How do the conclusions of radical feminists differ from those of liberal and socialist feminists?

ANSWERS

A1 Radical feminists claim that patriarchy — where the male is head of the household — in the personal and private sphere of home and family has always been the first and most important power relationship in the human social system. Hence their slogan, 'The personal is political.'

A2 The priority for radical feminists is consciousness-raising among women towards a sexual revolution that will transform gender roles and eliminate private, and hence also public, patriarchy.

A3 Liberal feminists ignore patriarchy in the private sphere. Socialist feminists argue that patriarchy begins in the public sphere and is reflected in the private sphere, so therefore an economic revolution is their priority.

examiner's **note** Do not confuse the entirely different political concepts of 'patriarchy', 'paternalism' and 'patriotism'.

Sex and gender

Q1 How do radical feminists distinguish between 'sex' and 'gender'?

Q2 Why does this distinction matter to radical feminists?

Q3 What do other feminists think of this distinction?

ANSWERS ▶▶

A1 'Sex' refers to biological differences deriving from nature, but 'gender' refers to socially constructed roles that both men and women internalise through conditioning from birth:

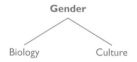

Gender

Biology   Culture

A2 Sex roles are more or less unchangeable, but gender roles can be changed. Patriarchy is therefore not immutable: 'Biology is not destiny.'

A3 Liberal and socialist feminists agree largely with this analysis but place less emphasis on it.

***examiner's* note** An androgynous model of human nature (i.e. a model that makes no distinction between male and female characteristics) underpins the mainstream radical feminist analysis of sex versus gender.

Contrasts and conflicts within feminist thought

Q1 Summarise the main differences between liberal feminism and radical feminism.

Q2 Summarise the main differences between Marxist feminism and radical feminism.

Q3 Are there any other significant schools of feminist thought?

ANSWERS

A1

Liberal feminism		Radical feminism
Individualist		Collectivist — sisterhood
Reformist	versus	Revolutionary
Focuses on public sphere		Focuses on private sphere

A2

Marxist feminism		Radical feminism
Patriarchy begins in public, economic sphere		Patriarchy begins in private sphere
Class inequality is primary problem	versus	Sexual inequality is primary problem
Class revolution		Sexual revolution

A3 'Black' and 'third-world' feminists stress the great diversity of women in and across cultures, and often accuse 'first-world' feminists of all schools of racism.

***examiner's* note** The feminist movement has become increasingly diversified since the 1960s. These divisions may have weakened rather than strengthened it.

Anti-feminism and 'post-feminism'

Q1 Which political ideologies are anti-feminist?

Q2 What is the main philosophical reason why traditional conservatism rejects the idea of equality between the sexes?

Q3 Is conservatism entirely anti-feminist?

ANSWERS

A1 Traditional conservatism and fascism are anti-feminist.

A2 The belief that society is organic inclines conservatives (and fascists) to regard the division of labour between 'public men' and 'private women' as natural, functional, inevitable and desirable: 'Woman's place is in the home.' Also, in embracing tradition, conservatives endorse the orthodox nuclear family and other patriarchal institutions that feminists seek to reform or abolish. Neo-conservatives in the New Right believe this most strongly. Essentialist feminists, however, also celebrate the 'unique nature of womanhood'.

A3 Neo-liberal New Right conservatives would endorse equal individual opportunities — regardless of sex — in a free-market economy.

***examiner's* note** Since the 1980s there has been a backlash against feminism, prompted by both the perceived successes and the defects of the movement.

 (89) ANSWERS

Feminism in the twenty-first century

Q1 Why does feminism seem to have waned since the 1980s?

Q2 Has feminism achieved its aims?

Q3 Summarise recent developments within feminism.

ANSWERS

A1 For some, feminism has gone too far in undermining men. The perceived extremism of some radical feminists has allowed simplistic stereotyping by their critics. Anti-feminist ideologies, such as New Right neo-conservatism and Islamic fundamentalism, have also had growing influence.

A2 Official UK gender statistics on pay, career opportunities, pension rights, health issues, domestic violence and so on suggest that even liberal feminism has not been wholly successful.

A3 This limited success has prompted the emergence of 'third-wave' feminism since the late 1980s. It seeks to reach out to young and to black women especially, and to be more flexible and less overtly political than previous schools of feminist thought.

***examiner's* note** Feminism is not dying — it is merely diversifying.

The origins of environmentalism

Q1 Who coined the word 'ecology'?

Q2 Distinguish between 'shallow ecology' and 'deep ecology'.

Q3 Why has interest in the issue of ecology grown since the 1960s?

ANSWERS

A1 The word 'ecology' was coined by a German zoologist and philosopher, Ernst Haeckel, in 1879.

A2 'Shallow ecology' is the belief that the environment should be protected in the interests of the human species. 'Deep ecology' is the belief that all parts of nature — human, non-human and inanimate — are of equal value and are deserving of equal protection.

A3 The issue has been given impetus since the 1960s by: deforestation, land clearance and species loss, overfishing, population growth, fuel depletion, nuclear leakages and toxic wastes, acid rain, the greenhouse effect, global warming, globalisation and growing concerns over food safety.

***examiner's* note** Ecology deals with the organism and its environment, including other organisms and general physical surroundings.

Anti-industrialism

Q1 Define 'industrialism'.

Q2 Why do most environmentalists criticise industrialism?

Q3 Do any environmentalists favour industrialism?

ANSWERS

A1 Industrialism describes economic and social systems based upon the mass, mechanised manufacture of goods rather than upon agriculture, craftsmanship or commerce.

A2 Environmentalist critics of industrialism, of both left and right, argue that its noxious effluents have had a damaging impact upon the ecosystem.

A3 A school of free-market environmentalism has recently emerged which is strongly pro-industrialist and argues that, in the end, all environmental problems will be solved by the mechanisms of the market. For example, as oil supplies are exhausted, the price of oil will rise so steeply that individuals and firms will be obliged to find other energy sources and to conserve oil.

***examiner's* note** Anti-industrialism has been a marked feature of the environmentalist movement, across the political spectrum, since its inception.

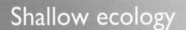

Shallow ecology

Q1 Who coined the term 'shallow ecology'?

Q2 Why is it so called?

Q3 Give one example to illustrate this perspective.

ANSWERS

A1 The term 'shallow ecology' was coined by Norwegian philosopher Arne Naess, who founded 'deep ecology' in 1972 and who also used the word 'environmentalism' disparagingly to refer to shallow ecologists.

Ecologism

Shallow ecology
Anthropocentric

Deep ecology
Ecocentric

A2 Shallow ecology is anthropocentric, i.e. human-centred.

A3 One example is the issue of deforestation. Shallow ecologists defend the rainforests on the grounds that: they absorb much of the carbon dioxide that is causing global warming; they may be a source of valuable new medicines; they help to prevent soil erosion and flooding; they are home to tribes whose cultures are being wiped out; and so on. All of these arguments centre on the instrumental value of the rainforests to human well-being.

examiner's **note** Most politicians and people concerned with the environment today are shallow ecologists.

Deep ecology

Q1 What is distinctive about 'deep ecology'?

Q2 What is meant by saying that deep ecology is 'ecocentric'?

Q3 Why do deep ecologists criticise environmentalism?

ANSWERS

A1 Deep ecology is the only political ideology that challenges the assumption of all others about the primacy of human interests.

A2 Deep ecology adopts the holistic, biocentric or ecocentric view that all living things are of equal value and worthy of moral respect in their own right, and that the human species is no more important than any other.

A3 Deep ecologists condemn environmentalism as no more than a form of engineering that treats the environment as a resource to be manipulated and consumed while seeking to minimise pollution and other adverse effects upon humans. They reject all conventional political philosophies as obsessed with mass production and limitless economic growth.

***examiner's* note** Deep ecologism aims to transform the relationship between humankind and nature.

Shades of green

Q1 Distinguish between the concepts of 'light green' and 'dark green' in the context of ecologism.

Q2 Give one example to illustrate these concepts.

Q3 In what sense are these contested concepts?

ANSWERS

A1 'Light greens' deal with the effects, but not the causes, of ecological crises. 'Dark greens', although still anthropocentric, go further in that they challenge the intrinsic virtue of economic growth.

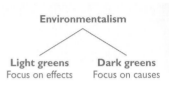

Environmentalism

Light greens
Focus on effects

Dark greens
Focus on causes

A2 An example is the campaign for lead-free petrol, which persuaded the UK government to introduce a tax incentive system — a success from a light-green perspective. For dark greens, however, this might actually have been counterproductive in encouraging more car use and fuel consumption.

A3 Many simply equate 'light green' with 'shallow ecology' or 'environmentalism', and 'dark green' with 'deep ecology' (see Numbers 93 and 94).

***examiner's* note** Whereas the distinction between shallow and deep ecology centres on ends, the difference between light and dark greens centres on means.

Greens, left and right

Q1 Are ecologists left or right wing?

Q2 In what ways are green ideas compatible with right-wing thinking?

Q3 In what ways are green ideas compatible with left-wing thinking?

ANSWERS

A1 Ecological thought can attach to the mainstream ideologies of liberalism, conservatism and socialism, but it also includes eco-anarchism, eco-feminism and eco-fascism. Greens may, therefore, be reactionary, reformist, radical or revolutionary. Anyone can be green.

A2 Right-wing ideologies often advocate ruralism, nature conservation, the organic virtues of land, soil and place, and the romantic idylls of pastoralism, which may lend themselves to environmentalist beliefs.

A3 Eco-socialism and eco-anarchism advocate radical decentralisation, small-scale egalitarian communes and grass-roots participatory democracy. Even the radical feminist movement produced a strand of 'eco-feminism', which argued that women were essentially closer to nature than men.

***examiner's* note** Greens usually like to reject the left/right model of political thought altogether, with slogans like 'Neither left nor right, but forwards'.

Environmentalist strategies and tactics

Q1 What strategies and tactics are employed by environmentalists and ecologists?

Q2 Give examples of the tactics employed by environmentalists and ecologists.

Q3 What tactical problems confront environmentalists and ecologists?

ANSWERS

A1 Ecologism is such a broad movement that its strategies and tactics range from peaceful to violent, legal to illegal and constitutional to anti-constitutional.

A2 On the small scale, individuals may seek to conserve energy by recycling, lagging their attics or switching off unused electronics. Green pressure-group tactics range from producing worthy research documents and lobbying MPs, to direct action, such as dumping waste outside the gates of Number 10.

A3 Much like anarchists, green groups often reject conventional organisational structures, hierarchies and leaderships, which may undermine their capacity for efficient organisation. Also, the use of direct action may be counterproductive in that it alienates public sympathy.

***examiner's* note** The divisions on strategy and tactics within environmentalism may weaken the movement.

Ecologism: some problems

Q1 What terminological problems are faced by ecologism?

Q2 What ethical problems are faced by ecologism?

Q3 What practical problems are faced by ecologism?

ANSWERS

A1 There are disagreements, contradictions and confusion over terms such as 'environmentalism' and 'ecologism', 'shallow' and 'deep' ecology and 'light greens' and 'dark greens'.

A2 Ecologism raises moral questions about the parity of humans with other species. This perspective has led some animal rights activists to commit acts of eco-terrorism, such as taking the lives of scientists who experiment upon animals.

A3 Some ecology movements have a romantic pastoral, anti-technology or anti-growth outlook, which may make them seem impractical and out of touch with the modern world.

examiner's **note** Particular sub-strands of environmentalism may have their own specific problems, e.g. about the need for a state; about whether a collectivised or a market economy is best; and about whether human nature allows environmentalism to be viable.

The UK Green Party

Q1 When was the Green Party founded?

Q2 Is the Green Party left or right wing?

Q3 Outline some of the party's current policies.

ANSWERS

A1 1973.

A2 The UK Green Party is left wing. As stated on their website: 'As long as the major parties continue to believe the Earth should play second fiddle to corporate interests, their green commitments remain just hot air.'

A3 Some policies include:
- Setting a domestic carbon quota for individuals
- Scrapping Britain's nuclear deterrent
- Limiting extractive industries
- Pollution controls, even where these reduce economic productivity
- Waste recycling and conservation programmes
- Opposing the illumination of Buckingham Palace on winter nights
- Opposing UK arms sales to Israel

***examiner's* note** The Green Party has no seats in the Westminster Parliament, partly due to the first-past-the-post electoral system. It does, however, have seats in the Scottish Parliament, the Greater London Authority and the European Parliament, as well as on many local councils.

Environmentalism in UK politics

Q1 Give examples of the growing impact of environmentalism in the 1970s.

Q2 Give examples of New Labour's environmental policies from 1997 onwards.

Q3 When did the Conservative Party begin to 'go green'?

ANSWERS

A1 Growing UK government recognition of environmental concerns led to the creation of a Department of the Environment in 1970, and to the Control of Pollution Act 1974.

A2 Policy examples include:
- Fuel taxes and road tolls
- Promoting renewable energy sources
- Waste recycling
- Publicity campaigns about energy saving

A3 The UK Conservative Party began to proclaim its green credentials in the late 1980s. Since 2005, the Conservative Party has put strong rhetorical emphasis upon a 'green–blue agenda', calling for a rigorous Climate Change Bill and lauding leader David Cameron's bicycle riding.

***examiner's* note** Greenpeace and the Green Party consider that all of the above stances are 'light green' — tough on carbon but not on the causes of carbon, to paraphrase — and that they ignore the big environmental issues.